Why You Need a Good Financial Advisor Today!

by

Michele Berson

Copyright © 2017 Michele Berson
All rights reserved.

No part of this publication may be reproduced, stored in a retrieval system, or transmitted in any form or by any means without the prior written permission of the publisher. The only exception is brief quotations in professional reviews.

ISBN-10: 1540838862
ISBN-13: 978-1540838865

NOTE TO THE READER

Thank you for reading my book. I wrote this to share some of my views, ideas, and more than thirty years of experience. My statements must not be used as specific advice. Even where my opinions or ideas may apply to your circumstances, they cannot take into consideration all the facts applicable to you or to any particular person or advisor. The information in this book is not a guaranty or any particular results, even if you follow the suggestions, nor a substitute for interviewing and carefully selecting quality advisors, and consulting your own professional advisors and for research and analysis pertaining to you. This book also contains opinions and forward-looking statements on various matters, such as what financial advisors do and what a financial advisor or the stock market will do. Not everyone will agree with my views. Forward-looking statements can be identified generally as those using words like *should, will* or other words that concern the future. Forward-looking statements involve risk and uncertainty because they relate to future events and circumstances and many factors can cause actual results and developments to differ from those expressed or implied by the forward-looking statements. Obviously, there is not and cannot be any guaranty or assurance of particular results, even if you follow the suggestions in this book. Lastly, I have begun each chapter with a quote from noteworthy person. The quotes do not imply any participation or endorsement by those persons.

Printed in the U.S.A.

Acknowledgement

The completion of this book was accomplished with the help of many people. They supported and encouraged me. Then they edited the heck out of this book. I will forever be grateful for their time, friendship, and inspiration: Joshua Markarian, Dr. Anthony Berson, Brian Berson, Martin Berson, David Gurnick, Marc Fein, Deborah Morgan, John Laudemann, and my clients who are so much dearer to me than being just my clients. You have taught me so much. With my thanks and love.

–Michele

Table of Contents

Chapter 1: When Smart People Make Bad Choices 1

Chapter 2: The Role of a Good Financial Advisor 7

Chapter 3: Types of Financial Experts 11

Chapter 4: Grow Your Money and Live Really Well 17

Chapter 5: Are You Married? 21

Chapter 6: Do You Have Children? 27

Chapter 7: Do You Want to Own Your Own Home? 31

Chapter 8: What Kind of Investor Are You? 35

Chapter 9: How to Invest Successfully 37

Chapter 10: Are You Planning to Retire Some Day? 47

Chapter 11: Is Retirement Running Away from You 51

Chapter 12: Making Costly Mistakes 53

Chapter 13: Being "Penny Wise, Pound Foolish" 57

Chapter 14: Garbage In, Garbage Out 59

Chapter 15: Legacy Planning: Passing Your Wealth to the Next Generation 61

Chapter 16: Getting Affairs in Order 65

Chapter 17: That's Not All! 67

About the Author 69

Chapter 1: When Smart People Make Bad Choices

"Great things in business are never done by one person. They're done by a team of people."
—Steve Jobs

I know you weren't expecting a test. I know you haven't had a chance to study. Still, please answer the following questions as fully and accurately as you can:

1. **Who are you?**
2. **Where are you today?**
3. **Where do you want to go?**
   - Are you twenty-five, out of graduate school, in your first career job, and earning $40,000 or more a year?
   - Are you thirty-five, married, with a child or two and buying your first house?
   - Are you forty-five and getting divorced?
   - Are you fifty-five and worried about having enough money to live comfortably when you retire?
   - Are you unsure about how to minimize your risk while maximizing the growth of your money?
   - Are you clueless when it comes to the best strategies to grow your money over time?

- Does money keep you awake at night?

Guess what—you need a good financial advisor.

Do you have goals for yourself? Do you have dreams? Whatever your age, your education, or your business acumen, you need a good financial advisor *today* to help you make those goals and dreams a reality. Why?

You might ask, "Why can't I go online, do a little research, and find all the answer?" If only it were that easy. I've spent over thirty years studying and working in this field, and I keep learning. I've found conflicting information everywhere, even from so-called "experts." I've learned one size doesn't fit all. But most of all, the reason you need a good financial advisor is because it's hard to know what questions to ask and what information to look for.

When you begin a puzzle, do you have a strategy? I've seen many different strategies from putting similar colors together to finding the edges first to create an outline for the puzzle. What's your strategy? Do you know the best way to avoid or overcome roadblocks in order to achieve your financial dreams?

Most people don't know how to manage the risks that are attached to money. Moreover, they may not even be aware of these risks. The right financial advisor, however, knows a lot more about that and other valuable tips that will benefit you in the short and long term.

The financial industry has a lot of information that most people don't even know exists. Did you know that when you receive an inheritance and comingle that money with your spouse's banking accounts, you could—depending on the state where you live—lose as much as **half** of your inheritance to your ex if you later divorce?

Some of us don't have a wealthy relative who's going to leave us with a generous inheritance, but we may be a stay-at-home parent with a spouse who has a great career and job.

As such, we may be eligible for half of our spouse's pension in a divorce. However, we need to ask these questions now and file the appropriate paperwork. That could be a significant amount of money to us during our retirement.

If one spouse takes care of the home and the other works outside the home, do you know that the stay-at-home spouse is eligible to get paid one-half of the other's social security income? The husband and wife will each get their full social security check. However, the other person will get an additional half. If you're now divorced but were married over ten years—and you didn't remarry—you may still be eligible for half of your ex's social security. These are just a few of the hidden gems.

Not knowing the emotional aspect of money can hurt you. Did you know that many lotto winners—even those who win hundreds of millions of dollars—**go broke** within just five years? Any guess why that happens?

That's right—they didn't have a financial advisor. They didn't have a financial plan.

Unfortunately, we're not taught at home or at school how to manage and grow our money—many of us aren't even taught how to pay the bills! So, it's easy to see why people don't know what kind of financial planning they need. They don't even know what questions to ask. This book asks some of those questions for you . . . and offers you ideas for a few solutions based on my decades of experience to help you make better decisions for your financial security. Please note that this book doesn't take the place of a good financial advisor but is essential to read before consulting one.

Have you ever shopped at Wal-Mart? When you first enter the store, you'll often walk past an elderly "greeter." Many of these senior citizens didn't take jobs as Wal-Mart greeters for kicks. Many took those jobs because they outlived their savings . . . or didn't have any retirement savings to begin with.

Scary, isn't it? Lack of knowledge, fear of taking the wrong step and, therefore, not acting at all, or believing you're educated enough to figure this money stuff out on your own are sure recipes for falling prey to bad investments, poverty-stricken golden years, and even villains. Fortunately, a good financial advisor can help you avoid some of the dangers of ignorance and inaction.

Primarily, a good financial advisor is a guide to help you identify the rules, the risks, and various money strategies. For some people, a good financial advisor is also a swift kick in the *derrière*, someone who helps them take the actions they need in seeking to protect and grow their financial health and wealth.

A good financial advisor will help you come up with a financial plan that envisions such steps as paying off bad debt, sending your kids to college, protecting your family if you suddenly die or become incapacitated, making sound investments, creating a strong and growing retirement fund, and much more.

As that great American sage, Benjamin Franklin wrote, *"If you fail to plan, you are planning to fail."*

Part of that plan for success includes hiring a financial advisor now, rather than later. A friend once said to me,

"You shouldn't be cleaning your house when it's burning down around you." For a while, I couldn't figure out what she meant, and I'm usually pretty quick. Now, after working with clients from the lowest to highest income brackets, I know exactly what she was telling me.

When it comes to your money, don't put off looking for a financial advisor until a need suddenly arises—the birth of a child, a divorce, an inheritance, a crisis in your business, change of jobs, a stock market crash, an unexpected windfall. Why not? Because then, you're **reacting** to something, rather than taking the steps you set in your financial plan. It's much harder to clean up after a crisis than to manage and perhaps avoid that crisis **before** it happens. Lack of time, fear, and stress aren't your friends. Remember that famous saying, "The best defense is a good offense" used in military strategy and sports? It applies to money, too.

Planning enables you to determine where you are today, where you want to be tomorrow, and what steps to take to help you get there. Your financial advisor will help you review where you are based on the information at hand, discuss with you options to get you where you want to go, and voice any concerns that may derail your plan. The steps will be set up with the thought of helping you navigate life's ups and downs and avoiding potholes that could damage your financial wellness. These are just a few of the ideas to be considered when creating your financial plan.

In addition to all the money issues that arise in your life, a financial advisor can help you with one of the most challenging aspects of successfully managing your money—fear. Most people—regardless of their education and their business background—are **afraid of money,** and they don't realize it.

Because they're scared and usually don't know it, they bring conflicting emotions to spending, saving, investing, and managing their money. Fear proliferates, as do prejudices, greed, hopes, desires, even fantasies.

If there wasn't an emotional element attached to managing your money, it would be easier to learn what you need to know and build the skills you need to manage your money successfully yourself.

But we aren't androids. We're human beings, and our emotions are mixed up in how we feel around money. This is often overlooked, and it's a very important reason why you need an expert whose emotions aren't engaged to walk beside you; explain the rules; tell you some hard truths that may save you from mishaps or, at least, reduce their impact; and educate you about strategies to take care of you and your money today and tomorrow.

Chapter 2: The Role of a Good Financial Advisor

"Half of the harm that is done in this world is due to people who want to feel important. They don't mean to do harm. But the harm does not interest them." —T.S. Eliot

People sling the words *financial advisor* around, but many of them have little idea what those words mean. What does a financial advisor actually *do*?

Well, do you have car insurance? Aside from the fact that most states require you to carry car insurance, why did you really buy it? Have you been in an accident? No? Then why have car insurance?

For your protection, safety, and security, of course. You have insurance in place so that, if an accident happens, you're covered. Because you're covered, you can drive your car with confidence, not stress, and get where you want to go.

That too is a financial advisor's goal, but on a bigger scale.

When I ask people what they think a financial advisor does, most of them say, "Invest my money." That's only a part of what a financial advisor should do.

The right financial advisor will learn about you and begin to help you create your personal financial plan, a plan that seeks to get you safely where you want to go in your life. Within that overall plan, you can ask for guidance on subjects such as:

- A healthy tax strategy (with the help of a CPA).
- A debt plan, including how to comfortably eliminate bad debt (not all debt is created equal).
- An insurance plan based not on products an insurance agent wants to sell you, but on the protection and peace of mind you need.
- A medical plan (created in conjunction with your doctor and an attorney).
- Short-term and long-term savings plans.
- A financial plan for your children.
- A retirement plan.
- An investment plan. You'll have the risk/reward ratio that works best for you.

Does that seem like too much for any one person to handle? Often it is! That's why many of the best financial advisors bring together a team of professionals working under the guidance and supervision of a leader—an overall advisor—to coordinate and balance your needs and strategies to help you create your financial health and wellness.

Remember when I said in the first chapter that most people don't know what kind of financial planning they need, and don't even know what questions to ask?

Fortunately, a good financial advisor does know the right questions to ask you. In fact, when you first sit down with a financial advisor, be prepared for a thorough interview that encompasses many aspects of your life and your finances that you might not have even thought about.

It's the financial advisor's job to learn the things that are most important to you, the things that worry you the most, your dreams for your future, your personal goals such as to visit a tropical island, to paint, buy a house, travel the world, marry, have children, go back to college, divorce current spouse, retire early, and even your business plan should you need one.

Then your financial advisor will show you ways to realistically meet your needs and desires financially, seeking to avoid the many potholes and dangers on the road, follow the rules that will guide your financial life, and develop strategies for protecting your money. They will also show you options available to maximize the growth of your money, risks that come with anything having to do with money, and ways to best mitigate those risks.

That's just to start.

Later, as you're living your financial plan, your financial advisor will help you navigate a myriad of changes in your life, your dreams, your new goals, your worries, your challenges, and your unexpected blessings.

The truth is, a financial plan is, in a sense, a living breathing document. It changes and grows as you change and grow. A good financial advisor will have the knowledge and flexibility to help you adapt your financial plan to best fit your life no matter what stage you're at, and to help you avoid costly mistakes that could derail you from your goals or dreams.

In short, a good financial advisor brings enormous value to your life and helps plan your best life possible.

Chapter 3: Types of Financial Experts

"A good decision is based on knowledge and not on numbers." —Plato

How is a financial advisor different from an insurance agent or an accountant, a bookkeeper, a stockbroker, or a lawyer?

Who is a financial advisor?

Pretty much anyone who wants to say they are. While most titles imply a certain level of education or expertise, people can call themselves financial advisors without having any specialized education, training, or experience.

FINRA, the U.S. Financial Industry Regulatory Authority, warns consumers that "Financial Analyst, Financial Adviser [*sic*], Financial Consultant, Financial Planner, Investment Consultant or Wealth Manager are generic terms or job titles, and may be used by investment professionals who may not hold any specific designation."

It's "buyer beware."

Of equal importance—and something that most people don't think about—is the fact that all financial advisors aren't created equal. In fact, each financial advisor is unique and thus different in some ways. Each financial advisor has their own investment philosophy. Some might be comfortable taking you on the "Space Mountain" rollercoaster while others might advocate the calmer "It's A Small World" journey at Disneyland/Disneyworld. Each financial advisor will have their own references and understanding of the stock market. Each financial advisor will have their own style.

Your job is to seek out and benefit from the right financial advisor for you. Look for and choose a financial advisor whose philosophies and style align with your own so that you can create the financial journey most suited to you. Remember, you're their boss, not the other way around, and you need someone you're comfortable with to be your trusted advisor.

Where do you begin? How do you find a trustworthy, knowledgeable, and skilled financial advisor? Should you, for example, only hire someone who's a "Certified Financial Planner" (CFP)?

In my opinion, No. Just because a person can pass a test—as I did over twenty-five years ago—doesn't mean they have the knowledge and skills needed to provide the best service to you. I know much more than I did when I took and passed the Certified Financial Planner test. It was my educational background and work experience that provide the knowledge and skills I use today when working with my clients.

I believe that a financial advisor's academic background, training, years of experience, results over the long term, and referrals from satisfied clients are more useful indicators when looking for the right financial advisor for you.

Fortunately, thousands of reputable and skilled financial advisors are out there, each with their own specialties and unique services. How do you identify the financial advisor you need?

You can start by asking a few simple questions:

1. What services and/or products do they offer?
2. How are they paid?
3. What do they specialize in?

Let me address the second question first. It's preferable—in my opinion—if a financial advisor is not, in general, compensated for *any* of the products you may need, be it an annuity, long-term care insurance, a tax filing, or even an estate plan. It's better if a financial advisor derives their income from your continuing financial health and success, which means that your best interests are their best interests.

As for the first question . . .

An insurance agent can say they're a financial advisor when really they're paid to sell insurance products . . . sometimes, as many of them as possible. Why? Because their commission on the insurance they sell is their income. But are the insurance products they want to sell you what you really need? Are there gaps you know nothing about? Do you know all of your options? A good financial advisor will discuss your insurance needs, fully explore your options with you, and help you choose products that are right for you . . . without earning a commission or fee on those products. In fact, they may help you work with your insurance agent in getting you the product they feel is best in your situation.

A stockbroker can say they're a financial advisor, but, really, their primary job is to sell you products in the forms of stocks, bonds, mutual funds, ETFs, etc. And for some stockbrokers, their commissions and/or fees on the products they buy and sell for you are their own income. Has your stockbroker reviewed the full scope of your financial situation, or discussed with you your short- and long-term goals? No? That's why many investors switch stockbrokers on a pretty regular basis—continual disappointment.

As I write this book, the laws seem to be changing to address if a recommendation is in your best interest and not solely a "suitable" product.

A lawyer who prepares your Will can say they're a financial advisor, but that paper on their wall is a law degree, not a degree in financial planning. Lawyers usually focus solely on the legal aspects and may not have the knowledge to take into account the tax or investment consequences. More clients than I can count have come to me after setting up a Living Trust on their Estate Attorney's recommendation. They usually did not discuss all the options and the pros and cons of each besides just having a Living Trust. And they don't understand any financial or other issues that could arise when a trustee of a living trust dies.

Education and full information are hallmarks of a good financial advisor. I don't claim to be an attorney. I do, however, have wonderful attorneys with whom I work on my team to provide the best possible information to my clients.

The third question you should ask is: Does this person specialize in a single financial area?

An accountant—a CPA—for example, can say they're a financial advisor. Accountants are concerned primarily with the tax aspects that include helping you reduce your tax burden in that particular year. I don't know anyone who wants to pay more in taxes. However, it isn't the role of your CPA to take into account your long-term financial plan. That's why a good CPA will often works alongside a financial advisor.

A good accountant is usually tax-sensitive. So when a stock you own starts to go south, an accountant might advise you to hold onto that investment. Why? Because the accountant wants to protect you from selling with a gain and possibly having to pay 15% to 20% in federal capital gains tax on the stock if sold. They can't review the potential drop of a stock—say down 50%.

Lose 50% of the value of the stock today or spend 15% to 20% and bank the gains today while looking for a better investment for tomorrow—Which is better for you?

If you want a specialist for a single aspect of your finances, then hire that person. If you want someone who can take all of these aspects into consideration—financial planning, taxes, insurance, retirement planning, trusts, investments—then you need a financial advisor, one who can successfully work with your *team of financial specialists* who are devoted to helping you create financial security.

How can you tell if you've found the right financial advisor? Pay attention to these two rules:

Rule #1: The best financial advisors don't force their beliefs about investments, taxes, retirement plans, etc. on you. That's like saying there's only one way to get from Los Angeles to New York—by airplane—when in fact you have several options: train, bus, car, or motorcycle. The best financial advisor will instead listen and consult to learn what is most important and appealing to *you*.

Rule #2: The best financial advisors learn *from you*. They learn who you are, where you want to go, and then put you on the right course to where you're going.

Sound good?

Chapter 4: Grow Your Money and Live Really Well

"Security is mostly a superstition. It does not exist in nature, nor do the children of men as a whole experience it. Avoiding danger is no safer in the long run than outright exposure. Life is either a daring adventure, or nothing." —Helen Keller

Do you want more money than you have now? Most people do. Do you have a vision in your mind of the lifestyle you'd like to have? For some, it might be an isolated log cabin in the forest far away from the pressures of the outside world. For others, it might be a Manhattan penthouse, tickets to every show on Broadway, and weekends in France. For still others their vision might be their own home with the mortgage paid off, a university education for their children at any college they want to attend, and a secure retirement . . . on a tropical island.

Do you have all the money you need to make any of those visions a reality? Probably not. That's where a financial advisor comes in. A financial advisor will study your current, future, and potential income sources; create a plan that sets achievable goals; and help turn that money into the realization of those goals.

The first thing to look at is where your money comes from. I'm talking about the income you get in all stages of your life. Not what you invest in (investments will be covered later). If you're like most people, usually, from the ages of 18 to 66, you're in what we call an Accumulation Stage. You're earning money, spending some of it on immediate needs, and—hopefully—socking some of it away to live your future dreams.

In the Accumulation Stage, your money can come from several sources, including:

>**Wages:** Paychecks from your job(s).
>
>**Passive Income:** Such as rental income from real estate you own, and royalties from something you created earlier, such as an invention or a book. Passive Income is the money you make while you sleep.
>
>**Business Income:** When you're self-employed and have your own business.
>
>**Investments:** Stocks, bonds, mutual funds, real estate, and other investments can generate income.

Then, for most people, the second financial stage is the Distribution Stage. This covers your retirement for life. In that time frame, your income can also come from a variety of sources such as a second career; Individual Retirement Accounts (IRA, Roth IRA, SEP IRA, etc.); a 401K Plan (known as a Defined Contribution Plan); Social Security (covered in Chapter 10); as well as investments held in taxable accounts titled "Joint Account," or "Family Living Trust," or "Personal Brokerage" and in anything from Certificates of Deposit (CDs) to real estate, stocks, bonds, and mutual funds . . . Get the picture?

So, how do you build financial security? The next step, with the help of your living financial plan, is to create a targeted and diversified investment portfolio.

Your financial plan may need to include a debt-management plan. Most people usually have some sort of debt; but not all debts are equal when it comes to creating your financial security. You can have good debts and bad debts, each of which may affect your credit rating in different ways and may help or hinder your financial health. A debt-management plan helps you reduce the bad debt and leverages the good credit to create your financial security. And that's just to start. Want to know more about the many minimal-risk ways to grow your money? That's why you need a financial advisor.

Chapter 5: Are You Married?

"By all means, marry. If you get a good wife, you'll become happy; if you get a bad one, you'll become a philosopher." —Socrates

If you're married, you need a financial advisor. It's as simple as that. In this chapter, I'm going to explore just a few marital issues that directly impact your money.

Many people now marry when they're a little older and perhaps a bit more mature, a bit more settled in their careers. Think about how vastly different life is for young newlyweds versus an older couple getting married for the first time.

If you've been married before, you may bring some financial resources to the new marriage.

Your Money: If you wed and bring some wealth with you into your marriage, either from your own investments or from an inheritance, work with your financial advisor to learn the rules and gain knowledge about the types of accounts that will enable you to grow your investments but also protect them if life turns in a different direction.

So, what about the wealth you bring to your marriage? Does it remain yours, or does it become marital property?

The short answer is: it depends, in part, on what state you live in. Marriage laws vary from state to state. Therefore, you need to consult with your financial advisory team to manage your money and protect it wisely within your marriage.

A friend of mine, in her late forties and married with two children, had inherited $500,000, a significant amount for her. Her first natural inclination when she received the money was to put it into a joint account with her husband. Her second thought was to plan a bucket list and start spending the money as if it were a never-ending supply of wealth like the goose that laid golden eggs. Thankfully, she came to see me. If she had made decisions without all the information I gave her, she could have had multiple regrets down the road.

As a resident of California—remember each state has its own inheritance laws—an inheritance is considered joint property in a divorce if you comingle the money. However, if you keep the money in an account solely in your name and don't "taint" it, it will be considered your sole and separate property. None of us get married, thinking about a divorce. That's why most have a sickly feeling if asked to sign a prenuptial agreement. I'm not advocating that; however, isn't it best to discuss the worst-case scenario with someone you love? Your marriage will last, but, in the event it doesn't, at least you'll treat each other with the same level of love and respect as you move in different directions. I'm not a cynic; I consider myself a hopeless romantic. But how many folks do we know who had an ugly divorce. Do you wonder what it may have been like if these discussions were handled correctly in the beginning of their lives together? Unfortunately, in case marriages don't last, we need to protect ourselves; leaving half of your inheritance, $250,000 in this case, to an ex-spouse can leave a bad taste in your mouth and diminish the lifestyle for you and your family.

Spending the $500,000 would be a blast. However, with proper planning, you can still have a great time as well as begin to create a comfortable future for you and your family, one that could include a secure retirement. That would be the goose that keeps on giving golden eggs.

Real Estate: You may also bring real estate into a marriage. Perhaps you already own your own home or commercial property as part of your business, or maybe someone has income property—a rental house, for example, that generates monthly income. I discuss real estate in more depth in Chapter 7. The basic rule is that if you owned property before the marriage and it remains your sole and separate property during the marriage, then, if handled correctly, it may remain your sole and separate property in a divorce. As mentioned earlier, if you comingle your stuff, it may get messy and become a costly mistake in the event of divorce.

A client owned rental property before she got married. During her marriage, she deposited the rent money she collected each month into the joint account she shared with her husband. During the divorce proceedings, the soon-to-be ex-husband wanted her to sell her rental property and give him half the proceeds, assuming it was his by right because the monthly rent payments were comingled in their joint account. My client spent almost $100,000 in legal fees to win the case and retain her rental property.

So, if you own some form of real estate when you marry, consult with the attorney on your financial advisory team. Your attorney may recommend you pay the mortgage and property taxes on that real estate out of a separate bank account that's in your own name. The same on rental property, your attorney may tell you to deposit the monthly rent payments into your own separate banking account.

Loss of Income: One of the greatest fears that most couples have is: what happens if one of them should be incapacitated by injury or illness and could no longer earn money? What happens to their family then? Will they lose their house?

For you, there's a good chance the answer is *No*. Why? Because in crafting your financial plan with your financial advisor, you may have built in *several* sources of income, not just one, such as real estate investments, or stock investments, or a home business. If you or your spouse is unable to work due to a medical condition or loss of job, you could still have two, three, or more income-generating sources to rely on. That's why you need a financial advisor.

Rules on Splitting Pension Accounts

Divorce has three separate sections: (1) how you split the assets, (2) how you split the income, and (3) custody of the minor children. I recommend you go through each of these separately, as divorce is an emotional and exhausting process.

Splitting retirement assets is possible without incurring a penalty and/or income taxes.

I've seen advice given, suggesting that when splitting a 401k, the recipient spouse is responsible for paying taxes and penalties when receiving his or her share. This is only half the equation, and it misses an important financial planning step.

The purpose of a 401k or Individual Retirement Account is to allow you to defer paying taxes today. The accounts also grow tax-free, and taxes aren't incurred until you retire (age fifty-nine and a half or later). Once you begin taking the money from your retirement account, you'll then incur income taxes on the amount you take.

Putting the money into a new retirement account will stop the penalty and defer the income taxes. Using a qualified domestic relations order (QDRO) is how you take advantage of this process.

In general, federal law provides that a retirement account may be divided in a divorce by a QDRO, and thus avoid the taxes and penalties. A QDRO works by allowing the retirement plan administration to carve out the spouse's portion and allow it to be moved into a retirement account in the name of the spouse.

However, if the spouse decides that they're not going to move the money into their own retirement account but, instead, take it out of a retirement account and spend it, then they usually will incur the tax penalty and pay income taxes.

The QDRO is a legal document, as is the pension plan, so don't do this alone. If not done correctly, it may not be enforceable or accepted by the IRS.

Chapter 6: Do You Have Children?

"You are the bows from which your children as living arrows are sent forth." —*On Children* by Kahlil Gibran

One of the first things most couples think about when they discover that they're expecting is how they can best set aside money to cover their forthcoming child's college education. Yes, some really do think of this issue that early.

But is a college fund set up in your child's name really what's best? Or how about a Coverdale Educational Savings Accounts? Maybe a custody account for benefit of the child? So many choices, lack of funds, and not enough time, oh my!

I'm serious. Setting up a college fund has been drilled into our heads for so many generations now, that most parents consider it a sacred obligation. They want their child to succeed, to do better in life than they have done, and to achieve more than they have achieved. Statistics show that a good college education will give their child a head start on that path. While college debt can wipe that out.

But should you set up an account in your child's name to pay for their college education? In my opinion, the answer is often no. Save for their college but in a different type of account.

Surprised? So are too many other financial advisors. Let me give you some facts to support my opinion.

Certain types of accounts earmarked for college may be of help. However, if you don't plan correctly, you may find that the account will reduce your child's eligibility for aid. If you have a lot of cash in personal bank accounts, this may work against your child in terms of qualifying for financial aid, but having a retirement account will not. If you're divorced, having a custodial account may affect how much aid your child can receive.

Tuition should not be the only expense considered. How about costs of living, books, travel, coming home on holidays, etc. When parents are planning college education finances, they're typically looking at using a combination of several sources such as grants, fellowships, and financial aid.

A specific financial account established in the wrong name or type to fund your child's university education could deny you access to many of those sources.

How *can* you help your child get the university education they need?

Well, the healthier you are financially, the more you can help your child. Remember, if you've funded your own retirement accounts this won't hurt you in qualification of aid. With the right start for your own healthy retirement, you may be able to reduce your retirement savings and help pay for some of those costs along the way.

I'd go further. Sometimes, having your child work their way through college and take out modest student loans could be the best road to their ultimate success. Really.

Interviews of graduating college students show time and time again that those who worked to pay for their university education have the greatest sense of satisfaction about themselves, their accomplishments, and the education they've acquired.

Yes, we've all heard horror stories about crushing student loan debt and the decades it can take a graduate to pay off that debt. So, in your financial plan, set up an account ahead of time that will help your child pay off that debt after they graduate.

Of course, financial planning for your children can go far beyond college. Do you have a special needs child? What happens to your children if you and/or your spouse suddenly die? Should you set up trusts for your children? If so, what kind of trust and what items do you want specified in the trust?

As you can see, if you have children, you need a financial advisor to help you address these and many other financial challenges and opportunities.

Chapter 7: Do You Want to Own Your Own Home?

"Money is only a tool. It will take you wherever you wish, but it will not replace you as the driver." —Ayn Rand

Are you thinking about buying your own home, be it a single-family house, duplex, condo, or townhouse? Your financial advisor will help you look at both the pros and cons of that decision.

Yes, there are actually good reasons to continue renting your home:

Saving Money. The cost of home ownership could end up being higher than the cost of renting.

Greater Freedom. A lease agreement usually lasts only one year or so. A mortgage lasts fifteen to thirty years. When you rent your home, you can pick up and move somewhere else, such as another neighborhood, city, even country, almost whenever you choose.

Less Financial Risk. A property owner usually pays for the repairs and some other expenses. Homeowners must bear these costs themselves.

The *cons* of renting include investing a large amount of money each month in lease payments without building any equity in the property so that it can repay you in the future.

Many renters also face fairly regular hikes in their monthly rent. The property owners could also decide to use the property themselves and evict you.

The benefits of owning your own home are many, including:

Tax Deductions. Interest you pay on your mortgage and the property tax you pay annually are tax deductible.

Your Own Castle. You are working your way toward owning a valuable asset that belongs entirely to you and may be a financial resource during your distribution years.

Individuality. You can make changes and improvements you want to your home without getting permission from a landlord (of course, you might need a permit from the city).

Home ownership also comes with its own cons, including a major time commitment— mortgages usually last from fifteen to thirty years—and some risk. If you want to sell your house after five or ten years, you might be "upside down" in your mortgage: you could owe more on your house than it's worth or than you can recoup when you sell it.

The outlay that comes with owning a house can also be a con. Do you know about *all* the costs of ownership?

Sure, there's the mortgage. You'll also have property taxes. You'll be required by your mortgage company to carry liability insurance. You'll have repairs to make, because something always breaks, be it a window or a water line. You'll have upgrades to make, everything from your water heater and furnace to kitchen appliances.

You'll have renovations to make so your house works better for you and your family. When your teenager starts driving, do you become a three-car family? Does that mean you have to enlarge your garage? Do you have an elderly parent who must live with you? They'll need a bedroom, probably their own bathroom, and maybe a wheelchair ramp.

What happens if ten years into your mortgage, you're suddenly laid off from work? It may take time to find a new job. This is a scary proposition when we still have to pay the mortgage every month. Guidance from your financial advisor can help you extend, refinance, or even use investments to pay down your mortgage to lower your monthly payments and make it more affordable.

When thinking about buying a home, a financial advisor will have you look at the long term, at what you want that house to accomplish for you, and then incorporate strategies into your financial plan, seeking to meet your goals. One of the first decisions you'll make is how to finance the purchase of your own home. Do you know the difference between what a banker does and what a mortgage broker does and which one will help you the most? A financial advisor does.

Chapter 8: What Kind of Investor Are You?

"To thine own self be true" —William Shakespeare

As an investor, these words, *to thine own self be true,* are essential for a successful outcome. We see two different types of investor strategies in the stock market: those who like to see an active (changing) strategy used in their investments and those who like to see a passive (develop the model, buy, and then hold) strategy.

There are pros and cons to each strategy, and both can be successful. However, people don't typically spend enough time in understanding who they are as an investor and then building the right investment approach from those strategies.

The investment approaches aren't as simple as they sound, and can often be confusing. There's the passive (also known as Index) approach to investing, which is explained perfectly by William F. Sharpe: "Indexed investing is a strategy designed to match a market, not beat it."

Two different types of active investing approaches exist. The most common is simply known as active management (also called active investing), which refers to an investment strategy where the manager makes specific investments with the goal of beating its index. And the second is a market timing strategy, which can be either day trading (where you buy and sell an investment usually within the same day) or a longer-term approach where you actively manage the investments but will move to cash if you feel the risks are getting too high. Getting confused yet? Most are.

A commonly asked question is: "When is the right time to invest?" But a far more important question to be asking is: "What's the best strategy for me?" Once you know who you are as an investor, you can put the right investment team and portfolio together and feel prepared to invest today.

What can also help you to stay the course with both approaches is a prepared financial plan. According to *Money Magazine*'s October 2012 edition, a recent study sponsored by the Consumer Federation of America showed that 50% of those with a prepared plan felt on track to meet their goals vs. 32% of nonplanners.

Chapter 9: How to Invest Successfully

"Price is what you pay; value is what you get."
—Benjamin Graham

If you're like most people, you've been tempted to invest in the stock market, to make your money work for you and multiply. But fear may have held you back entirely or in part. You don't want to wake up on a brisk October morning like your relatives may have done in 1929 or 1987 or 2008 and have the first words out of your mouth be "Oh, no!" followed by "Now what?"

For investors in the stock market crash of 1929, the market didn't recover to its precrash numbers until 1954—twenty-five years to break even! The stock market crash of 1929 was brutal, but it was hardly an isolated incident.

The S&P 500's Black Monday (October 19, 1987) was the largest one-day stock market crash in history and it still causes nightmares today. The S&P 500 (an American stock market index based on the market capitalization of 500 large companies traded on the NYSE and NASDAQ) also fell in value for three consecutive years—in 2000, 2001, and 2002—during a painful recession. If you had invested $1,000,000:

2000/Year One: Your account might have fallen to $991,000.

2001/Year Two: Your account might have fallen to $800,000.

2002/Year Three: Your account might have fallen to $640,000.

It would have taken you another three years before you ever saw a hint of profit. That's a loss of six years and a lot of money. If there were a better way to protect your capital and reach your financial goals, wouldn't you have liked to know that back in 2000, let alone in 2008?

What happened in 2008? The Dow Jones Industrial Average experienced the largest single day point drop in its history. The Dow had hit an all-time high on October 9, 2007 but less than eighteen months later it had dropped by 50%. Yikes!

A friend told me a story about a couple; she was in her late sixties and he was in his early seventies. The husband was in failing health before 2008. They sold their house and placed the proceeds with a financial advisor to make "suitable" investments for them so that they would have a dependable monthly income for the rest of their lives. When the stock market crashed and the Global Recession hit in 2008-2009, they lost **half** of their principal and had to drastically cut back on an already simple lifestyle.

What went wrong? Should you blame that financial advisor or the thousands of other financial advisors whose clients lost a significant portion of their earnings and principal in the 2008-2009 stock market crash? In my opinion, one of the root problems was that those financial advisors were not "registered investment advisors," people who are held to a different standard, who don't simply look to make "suitable investments," the standard one-size-fits-all system used by many. Is "suitable" in your best interests?

Simply put, their financial advisor had a different level of comfort when it came to the risk their portfolio was taking.

A registered investment advisor is regulated either by the state they're registered in or nationally by the SEC, and they have a fiduciary responsibility to look beyond what everyone else is doing on behalf of their clients to do what is best for those clients. There are ways to manage your investments for growth and reduce risk.

Unfortunately, this couple that was hit so hard by the 2008-2009 crash didn't have a registered investment advisor, or a financial advisor who would have created an investment plan with them that took into account the cyclical ups and downs of the stock market and weigh that against a constant monthly need for income.

Unlike more suitable investment advisors, their financial advisor didn't see well enough in advance that the stock market may have a significant downturn and, if it did, what the result would be for this couple. Nor did their financial advisor put protections in place should their investments start to lose significant amounts of money.

Instead of discussing a strategy that would reduce their exposure in the stock market, possibly set aside cash in case of an event like 2008, and addressing the client's personal situation and tolerance for market volatility, the advisor stayed with a strategy with which he was comfortable, a strategy he assumed they could endure. They couldn't.

Many investors and advisors in the financial industry don't consider reducing one's exposure to the stock market if there's significant risk that there may be a severe market pullback. They don't feel that's a sound strategy. And you may agree. However, if you don't agree, do you have the right financial advisor for your personal situation?

I believe that timed selling, when risks are high, is a vital strategy. I have worked with clients on timed selling and they have maintained and grown wealth over the long term. Not to mention they have slept better at night during market crashes. Why do I believe in such an approach? It protects your earnings and your principal before the market collapses. It also helps to reduce or even eliminate the devastation people feel when stock markets collapse and take with them the value in their accounts when the vast majority of stocks, mutual funds, and ETFs crash. Why lose all that money and then wait years to get your portfolio back to where it was before the crash?

Second, by having that cash from your investments on hand, you can then buy great stocks at lower prices when the market starts to rebound. Wouldn't you like to be a little like the legendary investor, Warren Buffett, and go on a bargain-hunting binge of a lifetime? History teaches that the market always rebounds; carrying share prices back up with it. But like debt, not all shares are created equal, and they won't rebound necessarily in the same way, or at the same time.

This poor couple missed out on one of the greatest bull runs in our stock market history! Their financial advisor had not turned any of their investments into cash. They had no cash available to purchase literally hundreds of solid stocks that had fallen in price to a fraction of their value.

What can you learn from this story?

First, investing in the stock market is risky, especially during shorter lengths of time. A famous person once said that the only thing he knew for certain about the stock market tomorrow was that it would go up or down.

Second, there are ways to reduce risk and make a significant amount of money **if** you have a capable financial advisory team. I mean a team that understands that one size investment doesn't fit all, a team that chooses investments based on **who you are**, rather than on what everybody else is doing.

Let me ask you a few questions:

1. Do you enjoy reading about stocks, bonds, and mutual funds?
2. Do you know how to identify the best growth stocks, the best times to invest in those stocks, and the best times to sell those stocks?
3. Do you have several hours each week to study the stock market, find new investment opportunities, and determine what the stock market will do next week, and the month after that?
4. Are you really the best person to invest your money in the stock market?

If you answered "No" to any one of those questions, then don't do this alone. If you answered "Yes" to one or all the questions, you may still need a financial advisor. You need their frank detached relationship to guide you with your own emotional attachment. In fact, you may enjoy consulting with your financial advisor even more.

The truth is that the vast majority of investors choose to buy a stock, not because of its historical price action and projected growth over the next year, but because they know the company. Perhaps they work for it, buy its products, read about it in a news magazine, or see it advertised on

TV. This isn't the best way to evaluate what you're buying. This method is always a huge mistake.

Most investors buy stocks because everyone else is buying those stocks. The "follow the herd" mentality means you buy into a stock too late and sell it too soon. You lose money both ways. Then we have the newbies who feel they can do this much better as a hobby than professions who do it for a living. That's like watching a moth go toward a candle. Not a pretty sight.

Are you getting the message? The stock market is complex. To succeed, you either need a vast store of knowledge and a lot of time to conduct the research necessary to pick the best stocks at the right times, or you need a thorough investment plan with the risk/reward ratio that works best for you. And then it still isn't easy. In my experience, the best person to assist you is a Registered Investment Advisor (RIA) with a track record of success, one who's part of your financial advisory team.

When most people think of investing, their immediate concern is: "How do I make a lot of money quickly?" They should, instead, ask: "How do I protect the money I've made and will make?" A woman went to visit her doctor after having surgery to remove cancer from her body. Her doctor asked her what she was worried about. Her reply was hair loss, energy, etc., and his response was, "I don't worry about that; I worry about how we beat your cancer. Keep your eye on the ball and don't lose sight of what's really important."

Anyone who has money—whether it's a couple of hundred dollars in the bank or several million dollars—knows the anxiety that comes with the many threats to that money, *most of which are not under their control.* Fortunately, how you choose to proactively protect your money from those threats *is* under your control.

Here's the best news I can give you in this entire book: your financial life doesn't have to be tossed about by the ups and downs of the economy, the stock market, human relationships, even death. You can and should plan today to protect yourself and your money tomorrow.

The following are a couple of common threats to your finances and your well-being, and a few solutions that you can implement with your financial advisor today.

Threat #1: Economic Recession—Anyone who knows about the devastating 1929 stock market crash and who survived the 2008-2009 real estate collapse, stock market crash, and Great Recession is understandably concerned about future recessions, not to mention depressions.

Solution: When you have a strong financial plan—and use it—a recession need **not** have a major impact on your money or your lifestyle. Yes, a recession could change things—you might go to the movies or eat at restaurants less, but, hopefully, you won't have to worry about losing your home. When you're not forced into a short sale, when the bank doesn't threaten you with foreclosure, when, instead, you have a stable household with your kids staying in the same schools, that relieves a lot of the stress that can come with a recession.

Here's an important fact you must understand: **The national economy is cyclical**. It moves continuously from trough to recovery, growth, and peak, and then into a downturn/contraction, which is followed by a recession or depression. The economy cycles through each of those stages continuously, but not at the same or even predictable intervals.

Historically, the economy **always** goes into a downturn, and when it reaches its trough, the economy **always** goes back into an upturn.

That means we will **always** have recessions. You can't prevent them. You can't fight them off. You have to accept that, during your lifetime, the economy will fall into several recessions. I've lived through six of them and I know more will come.

So, work with your financial advisor to try to recession-proof your financial plan. Build in protections or at least a plan for suddenly being laid off, suffering a drop in income, and the other troubles that could beset you.

I think one of the best solutions for protecting your money in a recession is **forward thinking**. You know now to expect hard financial times in the future, so plan for them today. I don't mean live like a pauper today and sock every dime away to help you withstand a future recession.

I do mean using your financial plan to create a balance between your dreams and your reality. I mean living **within your income** and avoiding bad debt.

Threat #2: Stock Market Crashes—Many people are frightened of losing not only their profits but also their principal as well in a stock market crash. Often, those people depend on their investments to provide a relatively stable income.

The most recent major downturn, the 2008-2009 stock market crash, pulled the financial rug out from under hundreds of thousands of investors who had thought the Bull Market party would never end . . . partly because some so-called "experts" insisted that the stock market could never again suffer a crash like it did in 1987, and partly because it's human nature to never want the good times to end, particularly when you're making money. As I write this, we're in another wonderful bull market that started in 2009. It will end; they all do. Will you be prepared?

We forget the past and simply repeat history. Once again, investors uneducated in the stock market are lulled into a false sense of security. Once again, they'll be shocked and hurt by the eventual inevitable stock market downturn.

Solution: Don't get me wrong. I'm an advocate of investing in the stock market... *when you're guided by a carefully constructed investment plan* that takes into account your needs, your capacity for risk, the level of reward you want, and the cyclicality of the stock market. In other words, you need an investment plan that helps to minimize your risk and maximize your profits.

Here's something you absolutely need to know: Remember how the economy is cyclical? So is the stock market!

The stock market moves continuously in an upward motion. It starts to climb for a time, and then it smoothens out and goes sideways before it pulls back once again and forms a bottom sideways movement. Some have referred to this pattern as a top hat. The Bull Market that began in March 2009, at this writing, has already lasted nine years. The crash will be frightening for too many uninformed investors.

Knowing that the stock market is cyclical, that crashes always happen, and that they're always followed by upturns, you can work with your financial advisor to plan your investment strategy accordingly.

Chapter 10: Are You Planning to Retire Some Day?

"If you're going through hell, keep going."
—Winston Churchill

Do you know how to manage your 401K-pension plan? When you retire and move your company's 401K into an Individual Retirement Account (IRA), that's a significant part of your assets. Congratulations! You've just become your own Pension Fund Manager.

Do you have the knowledge and skills to take on the most important job of your life? Do you know how to protect your nest egg for the rest of your life? Would you hire yourself as a Pension Fund Manager?

Most people planning a comfortable and happy retirement have several concerns, including how to set aside enough money for retirement and how to manage their retirement funds successfully.

Even if you're a multimillionaire, you should think about those things, too. Why? Because of some of the threats I've already discussed, from recessions to stock market crashes and catastrophic accidents and illnesses. Even though you've retired, life keeps happening, sometimes good, and sometimes bad. That's why you need a financial advisor.

One of the biggest worries people have about their retirement income is paying taxes on that income. I'd like you to relax. When it comes to resources like IRAs, defined benefit accounts, and 401Ks, every year you only have to pay taxes on the amount of money you actually withdraw from those accounts. You could withdraw just $10 a week from each account, and you'd only pay taxes on that $10 from each account, rather than on the much larger principal in those accounts. Your financial advisor will have you work with the team's CPA and together the three of you will select the most appropriate tax strategies for you.

One of the most overlooked and powerful strategies for postretirement income is Social Security. I'm not kidding. Too many people leave money on the table—a lot of money—because they don't fully understand how Social Security works and they don't know the rules.

Most people, for example, think their monthly Social Security checks will be a mere pittance and others expect it to cover so much more than it does. Wrong in both cases!

Your monthly Social Security checks are based on how much you earned when you were working. Higher lifetime earnings mean higher Social Security benefits. Thus, if you own a business and you try to reduce your taxable income to save on taxes, you're actually hurting yourself, because you're reducing your future retirement income.

Your age when you decide to start collecting your benefits also determines how much you'll receive each month. You can start collecting your benefits when you're sixty-two. I recommend waiting. Why? If you wait until you're sixty-six or even seventy, your monthly Social Security checks will be significantly higher than they would be if you started claiming them at sixty-two. How much higher? Those checks will grow **8% annually** as long as you don't file a claim to start receiving payments. Where can you get a guaranteed growth rate like that? The only two exceptions to waiting would be if you were in poor health or if you absolutely needed the money.

You can use so many more strategies to get the most out of the money you've built up in your Social Security account. A good financial advisor will know about many of them . . . along with many strategies seeking to protect and even grow your retirement income so you can pursue your dreams.

Chapter 11: Is Retirement Running Away from You

"The trouble with retirement is that you never get a day off. —Abe Lemons

I'm older, I haven't saved enough, and I'm fearful that I won't have enough income for my retirement needs. If this sounds familiar, then read on and learn what you can do (and what not to do).

I've watched a lot of older people who trust their financial advisor get talked into buying an annuity. Why? They're told that it's the best thing for them because it's a tax-deferred option and will guarantee a certain income at retirement. One reason the financial advisors like to offer this product is because of the high annual commission rate the advisor will earn for the life of this investment.

But why are you buying it and what are you looking for? If it's for the option to invest in a tax-deferred vehicle, then think again. You can put together a well-diversified strategic growth account with an eye on the tax efficiency (i.e., it doesn't have a big taxable capital gain distribution each year). You hold this to your retirement—over ten years away—and you save on the fees you will pay along the way. When you do begin liquidating, you can do so over time and pay the lower long-term capital gains tax rate. Do the math.

Also, bear in mind that with the annuity, your family may not get the same benefits. The money left over from the strategic growth account at your death will go to your heirs. And they get better tax efficiency on the inherited money with an immediate step up in value. So, when they sell, the tax isn't on what you paid for the investment but the growth in the investment from when they inherited it from you.

To summarize, while this may seems unorthodox, I would recommend the following:

1. Invest the absolute maximum in your 401K or other retirement plan, starting now.

2. If you're fifty or older and playing catch-up, you're allowed a higher amount to put away.

3. Know your options and reasons why you may or may not want to purchase an annuity.

Chapter 12: Making Costly Mistakes

"Experience is simply the name we give our mistakes."
—Oscar Wilde

During an introductory meeting with a prospective new client, the following questions came up:

- Why do I need a financial advisor?
- Can't I build my own portfolio and pay much less?

Those are really great questions and we are the first ones to admit, having reviewed many portfolios, that some investors are able to design good portfolios. In fact, we know that portfolio structure and low cost are the main contributors for wealth accumulation.

So, is the question really about advisory fees or, rather, gaining a better understanding of the benefits of having a financial advisor onboard?

Shouldn't the question be: "What's the real value of an advisor?"

The answer is simple: Behavioral Finance.

It's a term we use to help clients understand that the future outcome of their financial well-being depends on how they make decisions with their money.

What exactly do we mean by that? Take a moment to read and honestly answer the following questions:

- How do I know with certainty that my decision-making process is truly a rational one?
- Is it possible that my brain is wired to create and use faulty shortcuts, influenced by past investment experience?
- Would I benefit from understanding why the brain makes investment mistakes?
- What is the value of avoiding those costly mistakes in the future?

Below are just a few examples of the brain's systematic errors, best described with behavioral biases.

- **Familiarity Bias:** Investors have a bias toward stocks they know. Frequently, they favor their employer's company stock and take comfort owning large U.S. company stocks. In both cases, the results are poor diversification, higher volatility, and potentially lower returns. "Owning what you think you know" can be a costly mistake.
- **Overconfidence Bias:** This systematic error of the brain is very pervasive in people thinking they're smarter than everyone else. Being very bright doesn't necessarily translate into superior stock selection. Trying to bet against the collective knowledge of millions of other smart investors can sometimes lead an individual down a path of gambling away their fortune. Overconfidence bias is a serious threat to prosperity.
- **Hindsight Bias:** We all know that past performance is no guarantee of future results or, as we like to

say: "hindsight isn't foresight." Knowing that interest rates are at historic lows or stock markets are reaching new highs doesn't tell us anything about future results. Using the past to predict the future isn't foresight; it's still hindsight. Investors who have stood on the sidelines for many years waiting for the next big market drop in order to get in at a discounted price have to admit that hindsight bias can be a costly mistake.

So, the answer to the question, "What's the real value of an advisor?" is simply this: We provide the tools to help clients look at their behavioral biases and gain an understanding of how they make important decisions with their money—and how they may be doing it irrationally. Realizing our brain's own shortcuts and the impact it can have on our financial future is important. Having a financial advisor to prevent you from making costly mistakes in the future is invaluable.

As financial advisors, we might not always agree with you, but our first priority is your financial well-being.

The responsibility of a good financial advisor is to not only help you recognize behavioral biases and faulty reasoning but, more importantly, prevent you from making costly mistakes in the future.

Chapter 13: Being "Penny Wise, Pound Foolish"

"Money won't create success, the freedom to make it will." —Nelson Mandela

Do you really know how to evaluate the right mutual fund for your investment goals? To look at this question on whether you're being penny wise and pound foolish, I put the following statement to a test: Investors should look for low-cost, no-transaction-fee funds out of the same peer group.

To answer that statement, you have to consider a few things. Do you believe that all no-load, no-transaction-fee mutual funds are created equal? You may want to take a second look. How about the thought that it's better to pay a one-time transaction fee when you buy a mutual fund that offers a lower expense ratio? ⍰Ah, well, you may want to reevaluate this as well. Okay, then should you believe that a higher-expense-ratio mutual fund should be shunned for their lower-expense-ratio options? Umm, well, not always.

I looked at four random mutual funds in the same peer group.⍰⍰ I reviewed their actual performance after fees. My findings may surprise you. I've listed the four mutual funds below (names are withheld to protect the feelings of the loser funds):

	FUND A	FUND B	FUND C	FUND D
ANNUAL EXPENSE	.50%	.10%	.09%	1.25%
TRADE COST @PURCHASE	$0.00	$76.00	$0.00	$0.00
TOTAL FEE ON A $50,000 INVESTMENT	$250.00	$50.00	$45.00	$625.00

Which fund do you think would have been the best choice (five-year performance, ending September 10, 2013)?

No peeking! Write your answer first: Fund A, B, C, or D???

The winner is…. Fund D. Who knew? Buying a mutual fund with the highest annual expense outperformed its peer group with little or no trading costs and lower annual expense ratios. So, what should you make of this?

Well, we know that we're told as investors to be patient over time with your investments. Is five years a long enough period? Maybe, but to be safe, I looked again, and this time looked for ten-year performance of the same funds (period ending September 10, 2013). What do you think I found?

And the winner is….Fund D, once again, and by several percentage points.

Myth busted: Always using a low-cost fund expense ratio or a no-load, no-transaction-cost fund doesn't always mean you made the best choice on a performance basis.

My advice to you, the investor, is not to beware but instead to Be Aware so that you can make the correct decision.

Chapter 14: Garbage In, Garbage Out

"Successful investing is anticipating the anticipations of others." —John Maynard Keynes

So many of us are confused when trying to figure out how to invest our money for a positive return over our lives. We aren't asking for much. We want to know how much we need to save today so that we'll have enough money to pay for the necessities (not wants) of life—for as long as we shall live.

Seems simple enough to me. But is it? I read an article from our benevolent Vanguard Group, titled, "Revisiting the 4% Spending Rule," which addresses the question at retirement: Is there a safe amount of money that I can withdraw each year from my accounts so I never run out of money? Interestingly, Vanguard uses the 4% rule when, after all this time, I thought it was 5%. The short answer to this question after a lot of fine print and ten pages of explanation, is Yes!

Keep in mind that the article referenced was written by Vanguard, which is known as a passive, index-style investment company, versus an actively managed nonindexed-style investment company. Now, I'm not debating passive index style investing over active nonindexed-style investing at this time. It would be like debating Democrat or Republican and arguing that there's a one-size-fits-all approach. There isn't, and as far as I can see, never the twain shall meet...or agree.

With proper planning, a strategy that takes into account your comfort level over your lifetime, and the knowledge that—unfortunately—inflation is a fact of life, you can create a portfolio (index based and/or actively managed) that will allow you a reasonable amount of money to live on throughout your lifetime. And yes, a good rule of thumb for spending is 4%.

What Vanguard and others don't stress enough is that 4% of a portfolio that just dropped 25% or more may not be okay with you. You just got a 25% cut in your spending. Good luck calling your bank and telling them you're dropping your mortgage payments by 25%. But not to worry—the investments are expected to grow again and you should soon be on track!

The key decisions to make with your advisor, or with yourself if you subscribe to the do-it-yourself surgery kit, are:

- Am I willing and able to decrease my spending if my portfolio drops by 25% in any given year?
- Is there a way I can avoid dropping my spending amount and even possibly grow it over time?
- What is the period of investment returns you're looking for? How have the investment returns faired over the past ten to twenty years (as that is more in line with where we are today)?

Chapter 15: Legacy Planning: Passing Your Wealth to the Next Generation

"No legacy is so rich as honesty." —William Shakespeare

For years, the Family Living Trust was an important tool used in legacy planning by your financial team. One of the purposes of this Family Living Trust was to help you transfer as much of your wealth to your heirs by saving on estate taxes (a.k.a. transfer tax—transferring your wealth to the government).

However, when the estate tax law changed, it became less of an issue for estates valued below $10.6 million for a couple or $5.3 million for an individual because there was no estate tax. So, do you still need a financial team in legacy planning?

Absolutely.

Several areas are often missed and could cause issues for many families if not addressed. This chapter will shed light on a few of those areas, and I recommend you reach out to your trusted advisor and advisory team for more details on what to do and how to protect your family and your legacy.

Let's start with why you need legacy planning. Legacy planning is used to pass as much of your wealth as possible to your heirs and to continue to create financial security for your spouse and your family (heirs) after you die. I've found that, often, only one person in a family will handle the financial affairs and planning. If he/she is the first to die, then any planning that may have been done over the years usually goes awry. Why?

A recent article in *Investment News* by Liz Skinner states that statistics show that 70% of family wealth disappears by the end of the second generation and 90% by the end of the third generation.

The article went on to highlight one of the reasons for this, and the example made me smile: A financial advisor had helped his client with legacy planning because the client wanted to make sure his son was financially secure. He never discussed his plans with his son. Then, the week that the client passed away, the advisor got a call from the son wanting to know how soon he could have the money. He was building a pool and the contractor needed to be paid. So much for dynasty planning.

It's not surprising, as many of us don't include our grown kids in these discussions. And often, it isn't a two-sided conversation. It seems that talking about money has always been such a difficult conversation.

Many of us will say that we never had these conversations with our parents when we were younger. However, we don't have to make this the norm. I encourage clients to begin talking to their kids and teaching them what they know about money, as well as learning what their kids already know about money—and then planning as a family.

A client of mine had inherited money, along with his three adult children. However, his parents' planning and what they had hoped for their heirs wasn't clear. While the heirs wanted to honor the parent/grandparent, they didn't know what that meant.

Proper contingency planning is often overlooked and can cause havoc with your estate. Retirement accounts should have a designated beneficiary but often don't. Many clients don't realize that naming their trust to be the beneficiary of their retirement plan isn't a good idea, as it will cause a distribution from the IRA, and then taxes will be due immediately, eroding the value of the account.

A retirement account must name your spouse as your beneficiary. However, the spouse is allowed to sign and acknowledge you're naming someone else as beneficiary (such as your child or grandchild).

Name a contingent beneficiary(s) in the event a primary beneficiary has passed. Review the beneficiary information regularly, as death or divorce may change what's best in the legacy plan. The paperwork should be as complete as possible, so you usually need their name, date of birth, relationship to you, and social security number.

When a spouse dies, it isn't unusual for the other to remarry. In fact, 61% of male widowers are in a new romantic relationship within twenty-five months of a wife's death. These new relationships can create issues later for the combined families. One area of trouble can be spousal sharing rules and homestead rights, which, in some states, can trump wills. You definitely want to have a discussion with the estate attorney and your financial advisor about this.

Planning involves discussing the pros and cons to determine the right decision for *your* family. Talk to your team of financial experts, the estate attorney, CPA, and your financial advisor to decide what's best for you.

I hope this stirs some thoughts and discussions to aid you and your loved ones.

Chapter 16: Getting Affairs in Order

"In this world nothing can be said to be certain, except death and taxes." —Benjamin Franklin

When people speak of "getting their affairs in order" regarding death, what can we do financially and personally to make the transition to the grave easier for our loved ones?

This is a conversation that folks are usually uncomfortable talking about but is very much needed. I'll share with you some basic items that you or your loved one might consider when getting your affairs in order to create an easier transition with regards to your financial situation.

What I won't discuss in this chapter is: What is the Estate Tax? ⏵What are the pitfalls of probate? ⏵How can I control the distribution of my estate? These questions and their answers can be found by visiting my website at www.BersonMoney.com ⏵

Wills and/or Trust

If you have a will or trust in place, make sure that it's current and that if you've moved to a different state, that it meets that state's legal requirements. A quick story to illustrate the importance of this: My clients—husband and wife—for over forty years had a legal executed will that was put in place while living in California. When they moved to New York, they didn't check the laws for executing a New York will. When one of the spouses died, there was added hardship for not having a valid will recognized by New York.

Beneficiary information on IRA and other accounts

Make sure that all accounts have current beneficiary information, including full social security numbers. Incomplete names and/or social security information may require that you produce a valid will or go through probate.

Make sure you have funds available for immediate use upon death of a loved one

Upon death, if you're not a legal signer on the account, the account will be frozen, awaiting the correct documentation for the legal beneficiary and/or account executor. However, that takes time, and you could be relying on those funds to continue to pay the home mortgage—so make sure you've prefunded an account with some easily accessible joint money.

Create a list of important info, contacts, and passwords

Upon your death, your loved ones will need to update information that may require a password. If you have a social media site like LinkedIn and/or Facebook, they'll want to update the site and will require your password for access. What about your laptop? Where is the safe deposit key, and which bank and address? You get the picture.

A dear friend of mine who was my mentor, teacher, and, for a time, my boss once told me: "The devil's in the details." I want to leave you with that wisdom.

Chapter 17: That's Not All!

"The beginning is the most important part of the work."
—Plato

I've given you a brief overview of some of the reasons why you need a financial advisor.

Do you need more reasons? Well, do you have life insurance and long-term care insurance? Do you know why they're important and which products are the best for you? Do you even know how they can benefit you financially?

Have you inherited money? Do you know all the pitfalls to avoid? Do you know how to make your inheritance work for you to generate even more money?

Do you own your own business? If so, do you know the dangers of relying solely on your accountant or bookkeeper to manage your overhead, expenses, income, real estate, taxes, social security, and all of the other financial issues that accompany owning a business?

Do you know what happens to your money when you die? Do you have a correctly set-up plan to take care of your loved ones or the charities you care about, one that minimizes their taxes and increases their happiness?

Do you have the knowledge, training, **and time** to do all of this financial planning and management yourself?

No? That's why you need a financial advisor.

Your health and wealth are so important, yet most people spend little, if any, time or effort taking care of them. Only when the stock market crashes or they suffer something catastrophic like a heart attack do they take action. Yet, if they had only taken the time to properly care for their health and their wealth in the first place, they could have avoided the painful financial losses and probably the heart attack . . . and certainly all of that stress entirely!

When you have a financial advisor who's right for you, you're proactively taking care of your wealth—be it $150,000 or $15,000,000. Your financial advisor, and the financial plan you craft together, will help you manage your money no matter what life, the economy, or the stock market throws at you. You'll be taking steps to actively protect yourself and your wealth and avoid many of the dangers that are part of a financial life . . . which means living a happier, healthier, and less stressful life.

That's why you need a financial advisor today. I invite you to contact me at YourTeam@BersonMoney.com with questions you have on how to create your financial security in today's changing world. Also, if you liked this book, I would be grateful if you shared your thoughts on Amazon in a review.

About the Author

"Client education and comfort is my focus. My clients are partners in the process and feel supported and heard along the way, with no surprises when the market fluctuates up or down."

After graduating from UCLA with a degree in Economics in 1983, Michele started her professional journey in the corporate banking industry and built a full spectrum of client relationships, working with some of the largest corporations in the U.S. on their financial needs to the middle market arena and small-business banking arena.

As her industry knowledge base grew, Michele entered the private banking sector and worked with well-known entrepreneurs in the United States.

Michele continued to refine her focus in the financial planning field and became a Certified Financial Planner (CFP) and an investment broker.

At this stage of her life, with over thirty years of financial services experience, and after opening and operating several of her own businesses over the years, Michele decided the path for her was one of a financial coach working with and educating clients along their journey to creating their own economic freedom.

She enjoys working with clients and watching as they grow both financially and personally and achieve a sense of achievement and pride

When she's not helping clients, Michele is visiting her son, a student at ASU's Business School. If not at her desk or with her son, you'll find her playing with her dogs, a Havanese and a Tibetan Terrier.

www.ingramcontent.com/pod-product-compliance
Lightning Source LLC
Chambersburg PA
CBHW061158180526
45170CB00002B/847